THE
TWELVE
MONTH
GARDENER'S
JOURNAL

A WEST COAST GUIDE

THE
TWELVE
MONTH
GARDENER'S
JOURNAL

A WEST COAST GUIDE

Elaine Stevens
Dagmar Hungerford
Doris Fancourt-Smith
Jane Mitchell
Ann Buffam

Whitecap Books
Vancouver/Toronto

Edited by Elaine Jones
Cover and interior design by Carolyn Deby
Cover illustration/photograph by Paddy Wales
Interior illustration by Doris Fancourt-Smith

Typeset by CompuType, Vancouver, B.C.

Printed and bound in Canada by D.W. Friesen and Sons Ltd., Altona, Manitoba

Canadian Cataloguing in Publication Data

Main entry under title:

The Twelve month gardener's journal

Includes index.
ISBN 1-55110-046-0

1. Gardening––British Columbia––Pacific
Coast. I. Stevens, Elaine.

SB453.3.C2T84 1992   635'.09711'1   C92-091536-1

Contents

Introduction..........vii

January..........1

February..........13

March..........25

April..........37

May..........49

June..........61

July..........73

August..........85

September..........97

October..........109

November..........121

December..........133

Plant Wish List..........146

Friendship Garden Plants..........147

Vegetables and Herbs..........148

Propagation Record..........149

Pruning Record..........150

Pest and Disease Control..........151

Mistakes to Avoid..........152

Plants, Bulbs, Seeds..........153

Garden and Lawn Service Contracts..........154

Clubs and Magazines..........155

Gardening Book Wish List..........155

Gardens visited: Public and Private..........156

Nurseries and Garden Centres..........157

Introduction

✿ Keeping a garden journal is very rewarding. Years later, it will be an excellent reference, with information on all the smart and not so smart things you did in the garden from year to year— the successes, failures, purchases and gifts, what to do when, and where to put what. Like old diaries and photograph albums, a well-kept garden journal becomes an invaluable record of an important part of a gardener's life. ✿ This journal is designed so that it can be used for one year or several, as you prefer. Each month features one of twelve different plants, followed by a monthly check list of things to do and those you actually did, and a list of plants in bloom in our area, with a place for you to record what's blooming in your garden. There is room to record thoughts for next year, design ideas, garden notes and images, and reminders. The month ends with a gardening tip relevant to that month. ✿ The best way to use your journal is to think of what you want to do in the garden, and record it in a way that makes most sense to you. The different page headings should help you. You'll know where to make a note of the lilies you want to get next year, who gave you those Siberian iris, when you pruned the roses, what you did to control red spider mite, when you planted your vegetables, and so on. Sometimes you'll use it slightly differently than we suggest. For example, if you are in the early stages of developing your garden, you may prefer to use the Garden Images pages for pictures of gardens you like, rather than putting in photos of your garden in its present condition. This will inspire you to create the kind of garden you want. ✿ Other useful features are the spiral binding, which allows the book to open easily at any page, and the pocket inside the back cover for all the receipts, order forms, subscription reminders and other garden-related bits and pieces that might otherwise get lost or go astray. ✿ We urge you to use this book as faithfully and constantly as you can, so that eventually it will become as familiar and dog-eared as the Yellow Pages. Then you will find yourself constantly referring to it, because it will contain a wealth of information not to be found anywhere else. It will be both a record and a planner, a collection of memories for reminiscence and a guide for the future: the key to achieving the garden of your dreams. ✿ This is your book, and since you will be doing all the work, we dedicate it to you. Enjoy!

January

❁ January is an important planning month for gardeners, a time to pack away holiday decorations, pull out seed and plant catalogues, garden magazines and photos, curl up in a comfy chair and reassess the garden. This is the best time to plan structural changes, since leaves are off the trees and the garden is stripped to its bare essentials. You may want to add fragrant plants, and the gardening tips for this month offer some suggestions for every season. This is also a good time to start using the design pages to record your changing plans and ideas. ❁ The lovely autumn- and winter-flowering camellias, known collectively as sasanquas, are in bloom this month. Native to the southern islands of Japan, these hardy evergreen shrubs have been cultivated for centuries. Their shiny, dark green, slender leaves are used for tea, and their seeds and nuts used for decorative items such as beads, doll's eyes and rings. ❁ The sasanquas consist of *Camellia sasanqua*, *C. hiemalis* and *C. vernalis*, and their cultivars. They have single or double flowers in white or shades of pink and red, many with a delicate fragrance. They make excellent formal hedges and can also be used as specimen plants, either set in the border or in containers.

January Check List

Annuals, perennials and bulbs

- Order annual seeds from catalogues and plan flower garden.
- Check stored gladioli corms and dahlia and begonia tubers for rot, disease or insect problems. Order new bulbs now for spring planting.
- Check overwintered geranium (*Pelargonium* spp.) cuttings, and throw out failures.
- Plant lily bulbs in well-drained soil if weather permits.
- Protect crowns of tender perennials if frost is expected, and firm down roots of plants lifted by frost.
- Start cleaning up flower beds, removing leaves and other debris.

Trees, shrubs and climbers

- After a snowfall, carefully shake snow from evergreens to lessen chance of branches breaking.
- Ensure that stakes and ties are secure on climbers and trees, and that ties are not too tight.
- On a mild day, cut a few branches of early-flowering shrubs such as forsythia, Chinese witch hazel (*Hamamelis mollis*), or camellia for forcing indoors.
- Spray deciduous trees and shrubs with dormant oil and lime sulphur to kill overwintering eggs of insect pests and spores of plant diseases.
- Continue to plant bare-root roses if ground is not frozen or waterlogged.

Fruits, vegetables and herbs

- Plan the vegetable and herb garden, listing the vegetables you want to grow and when they should be planted. Order seeds from catalogues.
- Prune fruit trees and bushes and spray with dormant oil and lime sulphur towards the end of the month if the weather is mild.
- Plant fruit trees and bushes if the weather permits.
- Mulch or cover tender herbs if it gets too cold.
- Start lettuce and early greens in a cold frame towards the end of the month.

General garden activities

- Study garden layout and plan changes for next season.
- Sharpen, clean and oil garden tools and clean and service power equipment.
- Remove any accumulated leaves or other debris from the lawn and try not to walk on frozen grass.
- Create a beautiful basket for your front door or porch, filled with primulas, cyclamen, or other spring flowers.

What to Do

Done

January Garden Highlights

Bulbs

Crocus spp.*, *Eranthis hyemalis* (winter aconite), *Galanthus* spp. (snowdrop), *Iris reticulata**.

Perennials

Helleborus niger (Christmas rose), *Iris unguicularis* (Algerian iris)*.

Climbers

Jasminum nudiflorum (winter jasmine).

Shrubs

Camellia sasanqua, Chimonanthus praecox (wintersweet)*, *Cornus alba* 'Elegantissima' (Tatarian dogwood), *C.a.* 'Sibirica' (Siberian dogwood), *C. sericea* 'Flaviramea' (gold-twig dogwood), *Corylus avellana* 'Contorta' (Harry Lauder's walking stick, corkscrew hazel), *Daphne mezereum* (February daphne)*, *Erica carnea* (winter heath), *Garrya elliptica* (tassel bush), *Hamamelis mollis* (Chinese witch hazel)*, *Mahonia* ✕ 'Charity'*, *Rhododendron mucronulatum, Viburnum* ✕ *bodnantense*, V. fragrans**.

Trees

Prunus subhirtella 'Autumnalis' (autumn-flowering cherry).

* indicates fragrance

What's in Bloom

	Week	1	2	3	4

Thoughts for Next Year

Design Ideas

Garden Notes

Week 1

Week 2

Garden Notes

Week 3

Week 4

Garden Images

Forget-me-nots

Gardening events, guest speakers, television and radio gardening programs, book and magazine references, horticultural information phone lines, gardening courses, etc.

Gardening Tips

Designing a fragrant pathway

Fragrance is always an added bonus in the garden, especially if fragrant plants are located along a pathway where they can be enjoyed at any time of year, transforming a functional walkway into a constantly changing adventure for the senses. Here are a few suggestions for your garden that will give you fragrance throughout the year.

❀ Winter

Trees and Shrubs: *Hamamelis mollis* 'Pallida' (Chinese witch hazel); *Mahonia bealei; Sarcococca hookeriana* var. *humilis; Daphne odora* 'Aureo Marginata'; *Viburnum* × *bodnantense.*

Fragrant bulbs of winter and early spring: *Crocus* spp.; *Galanthus* spp. (snowdrop); *Leucojum autumnale* (autumn snowflake); *Iris reticulata; Narcissus* spp. (daffodil and narcissus); *Muscari* spp. (grape hyacinth).

❀ Spring

Trees and Shrubs: *Magnolia stellata* (star magnolia); *Prunus serrulata* 'Amanogawa' (Japanese cherry); *Choisya ternata* (Mexican orange); *Daphne cneorum* (garland flower); *Osmanthus* × *delavayi;* Viburnum carlesii. Hybrid azaleas of the 'Ghent', 'Occidentale' and 'Exbury' groups.
Climbers: *Clematis armandii; Wisteria* spp.
Perennials: *Viola odorata* (sweet violet).

❀ Summer

Trees and Shrubs: *Styrax japonica* (Japanese snowbell); *Magnolia grandiflora* 'Little Gem'; *Buddleia davidii* (butterfly bush); *Rosa* spp. (rose).
Climbers: *Lonicera* spp. (honeysuckle); *Clematis* spp. (some); and climbing roses.
Perennials: *Lavandula* spp. (lavender); *Rosmarinus officinalis* (rosemary); *Dianthus* spp. (pinks and carnation); *Hemerocallis* spp. (daylily).
Bulbs: *Lilium* spp. (lily).

Many annuals are fragrant, including sweet peas, petunias, stocks, nicotiana and heliotrope; and many easy-to-grow herbs, incuding sage, mint, thyme, marjoram, fennel, chives, and even parsley, are scented.

❀ Fall

Trees and Shrubs: *Chaenomeles japonica* (flowering quince).
Perrenials: *Chrysanthemum* spp.

February

✿ February brings with it the first hope of spring. Even in cold winters, when snow blankets the ground, some early bulbs and winter-flowering shrubs are in bloom. Many of them are sweetly scented, adding welcome fragrance to short winter days. Indoors, this is the time to start half-hardy annuals (see this month's gardening tips), and outdoors, when weather permits, it is a good idea to start clearing away winter debris. ✿ Of all the early February bulbs, one of the loveliest is the delicate little *Iris reticulata* with its sweetly scented, velvety, purple-blue flowers flecked with gold. Native to Turkey and Iran, this hardy little bulb has a netlike protective covering, hence its species name, *reticulata*. If left undisturbed, the bulb will naturalize well and multiply. ✿ *Iris reticulata* is an ideal choice beside a path or in a rock garden or trough—anywhere where it can be appreciated easily when few things are in bloom, and planted in groups for the best effect. It is especially striking when planted in the front of a border in association with other early flowering bulbs, such as yellow *Crocus crysanthus* cultivars.

February Check List

Annuals, perennials and bulbs

- If you haven't already done so, order seeds and start seed flats under glass. Sweet peas can be sown outside.
- Pot up cuttings taken from overwintered geraniums and water sparingly.
- Clean up flower beds and put debris in the compost pile, except for leaves from diseased plants, such as rose leaves with black spot.
- Cultivate the soil and weed thoroughly.
- Lift and divide perennials, taking care not to damage new shoots.
- Plant lily bulbs if not already done.

Trees, shrubs and climbers

- Finish pruning ornamental trees and spray with dormant oil if not already done.
- Prune summer-flowering shrubs that flower on this year's wood, e.g. hardy fuchsia (*Fuchsia magellanica*) and butterfly bush (*Buddleia davidii*).
- Prune summer-flowering clematis.
- Feed hydrangeas with well-rotted compost or manure.
- Plant trees and shrubs in good weather. Lightly fork soil under established hedges and give a light dressing of bone meal, well-rotted compost or manure.
- Continue planting bare-root roses and prune die-back on established roses in preparation for final pruning next month. Remove the old leaves and destroy.

Fruits, vegetables and herbs

- Complete pruning of fruit trees and spray with dormant oil and lime sulphur.
- Plant new bush and cane fruits and prune existing ones. Feed with well-rotted compost or manure.
- Sow annual herbs in seed flats, and sow parsley outdoors.
- Prepare vegetable beds by working in plenty of compost or manure. Lime two weeks later.
- Early salad crops can be sown under glass in a cold frame, and broad beans, leeks, radishes, and shallots can be sown outside at end of the month. Dates for planting can be advanced by two weeks if a cold frame is used.

General garden activities

- Power-rake lawn to remove thatch and moss, or hand-rake with a wire-leaf rake. Aerate with fork or aerator. Fill in dips and hollows in lawns with a mixture of topsoil and coarse sand. Apply dolomite lime at the end of the month.
- Check for slugs and snails before they damage emerging bulbs and new shoots.

A·C·I·D

What to Do	Done
Plant · New Dawn climbing	
· Autumn Sunset roses	

February Garden Highlights

Bulbs

Chionodoxa spp. (glory-of-the-snow), *Crocus sieberi**, *C. chrysanthus**, *Eranthis hyemalis* (winter aconite), *Galanthus* spp. (snowdrop), *Iris reticulata**, *Leucojum vernum* (spring snowflake), *Narcissus jonquilla* (jonquil)*, *N. cyclamineus**, *Scilla sibirica* (Siberian squill).

Perennials

Helleborus niger (Christmas rose), *Iris unguicularis* (Algerian iris)*, *Primula* spp. (primroses*, primulas and polyanthus).

Climbers

Clematis balearica, *Jasminum nudiflorum* (winter jasmine).

Shrubs

Camellia sasanqua, *Chimonanthus praecox* (wintersweet)*, *Cornus mas* (Cornelian cherry), *Corylopsis pauciflora* (buttercup winter hazel)*, *Erica carnea* (winter heath), *Hamamelis japonica* (Japanese witch hazel), *Hamamelis mollis* (Chinese witch hazel)*, *Mahonia japonica*, *Rhododendron moupinense**, *R. mucronulatum*, *R. dauricum*, *Sarcococca hookerana* var. *humilis* (sweet box)*, *S. ruscifolia**, *Viburnum* × *bodnantense**.

Trees

Prunus subhirtella 'Autumnalis' (autumn-flowering cherry), *Prunus* 'Pissardii Nigra' (flowering plum).

* indicates fragrance

What's in Bloom

	Week	1	2	3	4

Thoughts for ~~Next~~ This Year

ANNUALS *SEEDS*

Ipomoea
morning glory for metal fence in front

Poppies ~ White Cloud - 3' - sun/part sun - seed, uncovered.

Cosmos - lots of it
Stocks
Cleome
Love-In-A-Mist

Biennials
Canterbury Bells w/ pansys
Forget-me-Not, Royal Blue - SEED

* Rudbeckia fulgida 165
* Dutch Iris 79

* Hybrid Lily 26
* Orchid Beauty Gold - 76
* Anemone Blu Poppy 80

PERENNIALS   174-175
* Japanese anemone ~ fall   #
Delphinium 'Pacific Giant' or Round Table series
                plants
Lupine ~ dwarf, 'Gallery Hybrids'
* Sea Holly (alpinum) 163
* Phlox 142   Madonna Lily
* Balloon Flower - 70   Lilium candidum

BULB
Bloodroot ~ 'multiplex'

Borage, Fennel, Lovage, Lavender, thyme
chives, Rosemary, Cardoon (Cynara cardunulus)

Design Ideas

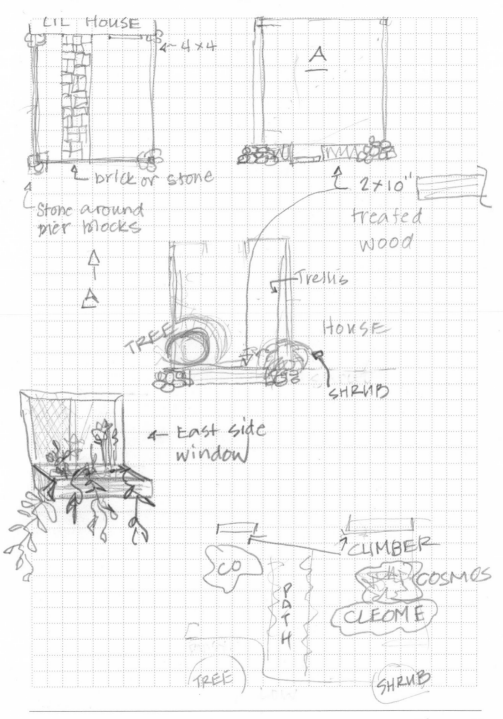

LIL HOUSE

4~ 4x4

A

brick or stone

Stone around
pier blocks

A

A

2x10"

treated
wood

Trellis

TREE

HOUSE

SHRUB

East side
window

CUMBER

CO

COSMOS

CLEOME

P
A
T
H

TREE

SHRUB

Garden Notes

Week 1

Week 2

Garden Notes

Week 3

Week 4

Garden Images

Forget-me-nots

*Gardening events, guest speakers, television and radio gardening programs, book
and magazine references, horticultural information phone
lines, gardening courses, etc.*

Select Seeds Antique Flowers - CT   www.selectseeds.com

Park Seed   www.parkseed.com - SC

Chiltern Seeds - UK   chilternseeds @
                           compuserve.com

1 tree
2 shrubs.

Gardening Tips

Growing half-hardy annuals from seed

While garden centres stock an ever-increasing selection of half-hardy annuals, there are still opportunities to add variety and colour to your garden by ordering from seed catalogues. Half-hardy annuals can be grown outdoors only when all danger of frost has passed. They can be raised under glass, starting this month, either in a heated greenhouse or a warm sunny place indoors, and planted outdoors in late spring. Many are easy and rewarding to grow, such as *Antirrhinum majus* (snapdragon), *Begonia semperflorens*, *Cobaea scandens* (cup-and saucer vine), *Matthiola incana* (common stock) and *Nicotiana alata* (tobacco plant).

Method

Use clean pots or seed trays. Three-inch (7.5-cm) pots are ideal; seedlings can stay in them until transplanted into the garden. Fill the pots with a mix of 1/3 sterile potting soil, 1/3 peat moss and 1/3 sand. Tamp it firmly into the pots, and top up with more mix if necessary. Stand the pots in water to a level just below the rim; when moisture appears on the soil surface, remove pots and allow to drain.

Sprinkle 6 to 8 seeds on the soil surface and cover them only as deep as their diameter. Very fine seeds need only to be pressed into the soil surface. Cover the pots with a piece of glass or clear plastic to conserve moisture, and cover this with a piece of newspaper. Turn the glass over and clean it every day, making sure condensation does not drip on to the soil and "drown" the seeds.

When the seeds have sprouted, remove the glass and paper and place the seeds in a light, bright place, taking care to protect them from direct sunlight for the first few days. When the first pair of true leaves appear, thin out the weaker seedlings, leaving 2 or 3 plants in each pot. Turn pots daily to prevent the seedlings from bending towards the light. It is best to water with a hand-pumped spray bottle, and make sure to keep the soil moist.

Unfortunately, the conditions that promote germination are also ideal for the growth of a fungal disease referred to as "damping off." To help prevent this, avoid overcrowding the seedlings so they have good air circulation, and do not water with cold or dirty water.

After one month indoors the plants should be ready to be hardened off. Set them out during the day in a sheltered spot, away from direct sunlight, and bring them in again at night; if you have a cold frame, place the plants in it.

After all danger of frost is over, and when the plants look strong and healthy, they are ready to be transplanted directly into the garden. The earliest safe time to do this in most areas on the West Coast is May 15.

March

❂ March is one of the most critical months of all in the garden. Slugs and snails are back in full force, nibbling at tender young shoots as they emerge from the ground; cutworms, aphids, root weevils and many other garden pests are waiting to pounce on spring growth; and diseases such as black spot and powdery mildew may be passed on from last year's affected foliage unless cleared away. This is clean-up time; any effort you put in now will pay dividends all year long and there are some simple tips to help you at the end of the March section. ❂ Of all the woodland bulbs that flower now, erythroniums are some of the prettiest. Several species are native to the West Coast, such as *Erythronium revolutum*, the trout or coast fawn lily, which can be found all the way from British Columbia to the woodlands of Northern California. ❂ It has graceful pink flowers borne on 12-inch (30-cm) stems above interestingly mottled leaves. It adapts well to garden cultivation, especially when planted in a shady location, either in a rock garden, under a shrub or in a mixed border. Erythroniums are most appealing when planted in drifts in the dappled sunlight of a woodland garden, and multiply well if left undisturbed.

March Check List

Annuals, perennials and bulbs

- Continue to clear and weed flower beds, and mulch with well-rotted compost or mushroom manure.
- Plant summer bulbs of lilies, acidanthera, and nerines, and corms of gladioli.
- Continue to lift and divide perennials and plant new ones.
- Deadhead and feed spring bulbs when they have finished flowering.
- Harden off hardy annual seedlings in cold frame or sow in ground.
- Sow tender annuals indoors.
- Pot up rooted cuttings and overwintered tuberous begonias.

Trees, shrubs and climbers

- Prune early-blooming deciduous shrubs, such as forsythia, after flowering.
- Prune grey-leafed plants like lavender, lavender cotton and senecio.
- After the fifteenth of the month, prune hybrid tea and floribunda roses.
- If shrubs or trees are to be moved, this is a good month to do so.
- Evergreens, including hedges, should be planted now and mulched with well-rotted compost or manure. Prune out any winter-damaged hedging.

Fruits, vegetables and herbs

- Complete pruning of tree and bush fruits by the end of the month.
- Train tayberry, loganberry or blackberry branches to wire or fence supports.
- March 1 to 15, begin to sow radish, garlic and broad beans. March 16 to 31, begin successive sowings of peas, spinach, leaf lettuce, Chinese vegetables, onion sets, turnips and shallots. Sow tomatoes indoors.
- Plant new strawberry plants and feed established plants.
- Feed rhubarb well with rich organic material.
- Sow seeds of annual herbs, and prune established herbs such as sage, rue, and thyme if they have become leggy.

General garden activities

- Seed or sod new lawns and repair worn patches on existing ones. Edge lawns and begin mowing when grass is 3 inches (8 cm) high. Aerate and apply dolomite lime if not already done.
- Remove winter mulches and compost them.

What to Do	Done
· Plant/mulch tulip bed	
· Weed, mulch, plant magnolia b	
· Weed, prune rose bed	
· Divide, weed perennial b.	
· Woodland area … plant s.s.	
· Plant lily/rose gardens	
· Clean area for wildflowers	
· Prepare lawn for seeding	
Plan for new roses	

March Garden Highlights

Bulbs

Anemone blanda (windflower), *Chionodoxa* spp. (glory-of-the-snow), *Crocus* spp.*, *Cyclamen coum, Erythronium oregonum* (Easter lily, dog-tooth violet), *Hyacinthus* spp. (hyacinth)*, *Iris reticulata**, *Leucojum vernum* (spring snowflake), *Narcissus* spp. (daffodils and narcissus), *Scilla* spp. (squill), *Tulipa* spp. (tulips).

Perennials

Alyssum montanum (perennial alyssum) and *Aurinia saxatilis* (formerly *Alyssum saxatilis*), *Aubrieta deltoidea* (aubrietia), *Bergenia* spp. (bergenia), *Doronicum* spp. (leopard's bane), *Primula* spp. (primroses), *P. vulgaris* (English primrose)*, *Pulmonaria* spp. (lungwort), *Viola odorata* (sweet violet)*.

Climbers

Clematis armandii (evergreen clematis)*.

Shrubs

Camellia japonica (camellia), *Cornus mas* (Cornelian cherry), *Daphne odora* (winter daphne)*, *Forsythia* spp., *Magnolia stellata* (star magnolia)*, *Pieris* spp. (lily-of-the-valley shrub), *Rhododendron* 'Cilpinense', *Rhododendron* 'Christmas Cheer'.

Trees

Prunus × *blireiana* (flowering plum), *Prunus* 'Pissardii Nigra' (flowering plum), *P.* 'Accolade' (flowering cherry), *P. subhirtella* 'Pendula' (flowering cherry), *P.* × *yedoensis* (flowering cherry)*.

* indicates fragrance

What's in Bloom

	Week	1	2	3	4

Thoughts for Next Year

Did no rose pruning this spring. May
want to do so next spring. They are
currently leggy./2001

Design Ideas

Garden Notes

Week 1

Week 2

Garden Notes

Week 3

Week 4

Garden Images

Forget-me-nots

Gardening events, guest speakers, television and radio gardening programs, book and magazine references, horticultural information phone lines, gardening courses, etc.

Gardening Tips

Keeping the garden healthy

There's no great secret to having a healthy, productive garden. All it takes is common sense, a basic knowledge of good gardening practices, and consistent effort. This means keeping the garden clean, enriching the soil regularly, and treating insects and diseases in an environmentally responsible, safe way so that you can maintain the health and ecological balance of your garden. A common-sense approach to gardening can eliminate the need for toxic chemicals by creating a healthy balance between the pests and predators, diseases and biologically-safe controls.

An ounce of prevention

- Buy only healthy plants and good-quality seeds and bulbs. Look for disease-resistant cultivars.
- Make sure the plants you buy are suited to the sites you choose for them, and that all their requirements are met. A plant under stress is much more susceptible to pests and disease.
- Keep the garden tidy and weed free. Rotting plants can be a source of infection and will attract pests to the garden. Clean up and destroy all infected plant material.
- Prune out dead and diseased branches, and ensure that trees and shrubs have adequate ventilation by removing overcrowded and crossing branches.
- Prepare the ground properly when planting or sowing, and follow instructions carefully for any given plant.
- If a plant is not thriving, and is diseased or continually attacked by pests, get rid of it and plant something else.

Winter moth alert

These bright-green caterpillars are a major problem in some areas of the West Coast. They are nearly one inch (2 cm) long, with whitish stripes on each side of their bodies. They attack a wide variety of deciduous trees and shrubs, beginning in April and May. They feed on leaves and buds, often "sewing" the leaves together. Young caterpillars are carried on the wind, and drift a considerable distance on silken threads, so protected trees can become infested from neglected trees in the neighbouring area. Male moths are brownish-grey, with a wingspan of about 1 1/2 inches (4 cm). Females are wingless. Unfortunately nothing can be done about controlling the winter moth until the fall. (See October gardening tips.)

April

❈ Spring is now in full flower—a good time to run a critical eye over your garden colour scheme and make sure that colours blend and harmonize, rather than fight with each other. Should the red tulips be moved away from the purple rhododendron? Do the red, purple, pink and yellow rhododendrons show to advantage when they are all clumped together? Use these pages to do the planning and make notes and reminders. This is also a great time to prepare beds for late spring vegetables and plant some unusual salad greens, using the suggestions in this month's gardening tips. ❈ Of the many clematis in bloom this month, one especially attractive species is *Clematis alpina*, with its dainty, satiny-blue nodding flowers and white stamens. It grows wild in alpine areas of Europe and Northeast Asia, and is commonly known as alpine virgin's bower.

C. alpina is an ideal choice for a small garden; it grows only to a height of 6 feet (2 m) and looks equally attractive growing through a shrub, up a trellis or as ground cover. ❈ Although its main flowering is in spring, it will often flower again in the late summer, although not as profusely. The flowers give way to fluffy, silky seed heads, which make an interesting addition to any flower arrangement.

April Check List

Annuals, perennials and bulbs

- Deadhead daffodils but leave seed pods on squills and grape hyacinths to seed themselves. Don't remove foliage until it has started to yellow.
- Divide up primroses and polyanthus after flowering.
- Edge flower beds, weed well and check carefully for invading pests and diseases.
- Stake perennials that need it, and mulch perennials if not already done.
- Continue to sow seeds of hardy annuals in ground.

Trees, shrubs and climbers

- Rose pruning should be completed by the beginning of the month. Mulch with mushroom manure or well-rotted compost. Check for aphids and rub off, or use an insecticidal soap.
- Shear winter-flowering heathers after flowering.
- Continue planting trees and shrubs.
- Prune early-blooming shrubs such as *Spiraea thunbergii* and *Forsythia* spp. after flowering.
- Evergreen and conifer hedges can be clipped now.
- Check vines growing on the house to make sure they are not invading window frames or working their way under gutters and shingles.

Fruits, vegetables and herbs

- April 1 to 15, plant early potatoes, green onions, bulb onions, kohlrabi, cabbage and leeks.
- April 16 to 30, sow beets, carrots, Swiss chard, broccoli, cauliflower, parsnip, kale and lettuce. Set out earlier-sown vegetables from the cold frame.
- Sow zucchini, cucumbers and tomatoes indoors in a sunny window or a cold frame.
- Keep vegetable garden well weeded; watch for signs of pests and diseases.
- Plant out new strawberry plants.

Other garden activities

- Continue preparing new lawns and repairing worn patches on existing ones. The first three lawn mowings should be done with the blades set higher than usual.
- Aerate lawn if not already done.
- Start planting water plants in pool.
- Turn compost and keep it moist.

What to Do	Done
Mulch roses w/ mushroom manure	
Divide primroses	
Stake or tie perennials	
Deadhead daffodils	
Prune laurel	
Shear heathers if ready	
Plant trees	

April Garden Highlights

Bulbs

Anemone blanda (windflower), *Erythronium* spp. (dog-tooth violet or fawn lily), *Fritillaria imperialis* (crown imperial lily), *Ipheion uniflorum* (star flower), *Muscari* spp. (grape hyacinth), *Narcissus* spp. (daffodil)*, *Puschkinia scilloides**, *Scilla* spp. (squill), *Trillium*, *Tulipa* spp. (tulips).

Perennials

Alyssum montanum (perennial alyssum) and *Aurinia saxatilis* (formerly *Alyssum saxatilis*), *Anemone pulsatilla* (pasqueflower), *Aubrieta deltoidea* (aubrietia), *Bellis perennis* (English daisy), *Bergenia* spp., *Dicentra* spp. (bleeding heart), *Epimedium* (barrenwort), *Helleborus orientalis* (Lenten rose), *Myosotis* spp. (forget-me-not), *Omphaloides* (navelwort), *Polygonatum* × *hybridum* (Solomon's seal), *Pulmonaria* spp. (lungwort), *Sanguinaria canadensis* (bloodroot).

Climbers

Clematis alpina, *Clematis armandii* (evergreen clematis)*.

Shrubs

Berberis darwinii (Darwin's barberry), *Camellia japonica*, *Chaenomeles* spp. (Japanese flowering quince), *Cytisus praecox* (broom)*, *Daphne cneorum* (garland daphne)*, *Exochorda* spp. (pearlbush), *Kerria japonica*, *Magnolia stellata* (star magnolia), *Osmanthus* × *burkwoodii**, *O. delavayi*, *Rhododendron* spp. and hybrids (rhododendrons and azaleas), *Spiraea* × *arguta* (bridal wreath), *S. prunifolia* (bridal wreath), *Viburnum* spp.

Trees

*Magnolia denudata**, *M. soulangeana*, *Malus* spp. (flowering crabapple), *Prunus* spp. (flowering cherry).

* indicates fragrance

What's in Bloom

	Week	1	2	3	4
Tulips ~ all			✓	✓	
Magnolia		✓	✓	✓	
Rhodos				✓	
Hellebore		✓	✓	✓	
Forget-me-not					
Camellias ~ red first		✓	✓ W	✓ W	

Thoughts for Next Year

Remove red tulips from front garden, on sidewalk. (marked with stake) Replace with purple & white tulips.

Design Ideas

Garden Notes

Week 1

Week 2

Garden Notes

Week 3

Week 4

Garden Images

Forget-me-nots

Gardening events, guest speakers, television and radio gardening programs, book and magazine references, horticultural information phone lines, gardening courses, etc.

Gardening Tips

Grow your own salad greens

Today there is an increased appreciation for wholesome, fresh, uncooked foods, and many gourmet stores carry ready-prepared salad mixes of unusual greens, herbs and flowers. These are expensive, however, and it is easy and fun to grow your own ingredients. It's best to plan for a succession of plantings, and select cultivars grown by local companies, such as Territorial Seeds. Here are some ideas for creating a salad patch that is both visually appealing and good to eat.

The ideal spot for the bed is near the house, in a spot that receives good morning sun and is easy to water. Raise the bed so that it will drain well; dig the soil twice, to a depth of one foot (30 cm) and add large amounts of organic matter (compost, well-rotted manure, liquid seaweed). Mark out the areas to be planted, so that seed can be sown in patterns and interesting shapes, and make sure the patch is weed-free.

Seed companies sell many interesting varieties of greens. The following selection will give you a good salad mix.

Lettuces: a blend of varieties could include 'Buttercrunch', 'Red Sails', 'Slobolt', 'Salad Bowls' and 'Valmaine'.

Spinach: 'Mazurka' has large, dark leaves, a sweet, mild flavour, and, unlike most other varieties of spinach, can be grown in summer.

Arugula: dark green, pungently nutty-flavoured leaves.

Cresses: sharp, crisp flavours. Grows best in cool conditions.

Maché or corn salad: unusual tasting and frost-hardy.

Mustard and oriental greens: useful for spring, fall and winter salads. 'Mizuna' is a vigorous grower with frilly leaves and a mild, sweet flavour.

Herbs: the leaves, flowers and seeds of culinary herbs are all edible and make an interesting addition to salad. Good ones to begin with are basil, coriander, dill, fennel, parsley, sage, rosemary, salad burnet, thyme, lovage and mint.

Flowers: good ones to try include borage and chive flowers, Johnny jump-ups, rose petals and nasturtiums.

One tablespoon (50 mL) of seeds should cover a square yard (square metre) of soil. Time successive sowings from the last frost in spring through to August plantings for fall and winter salads.

It's best to harvest regularly, cutting young, new leaves close to the ground so that the plant will sprout a second and third time. Amend the soil with fish fertilizer or canola seed meal between cuttings, and water well. Early morning harvests yield the most succulent leaves.

May

❈ May is a lovely time in the garden. Early summer perennials are just coming into bloom, late bulbs are still flowering, and horse chestnut, dogwood and crab-apple trees brighten city streets. Basic care and maintenance, such as staking and deadheading, are important now. By about the middle of this month all danger of frost is past, and it's time to plant out your seedlings—the half-hardy perennials and tender herbs and vegetables. If you grow plants from seed, a cold frame, such as the one described in the gardening tips for this month, is very useful year-round, and is easy to make.

❈ An attractive perennial that blooms this month is the columbine, with its nodding, spurred blooms and grey-green foliage. Several species of columbine (*Aquilegia* spp.) are native to North America, and bloom from May to August in shady, moist places. One of the most striking is A. *canadensis* with lemon-yellow flowers and bright red spurs. Like all columbines it grows easily from seed and is an excellent plant for a lightly shaded area in the garden, combining well with other woodland plants such as cranesbill (*Geranium* spp.) and *Epimedium* spp.

May Check List

Annuals, perennials and bulbs

- Buy bedding plants and plant out after the fifteenth of the month. Plant up tubs, hanging baskets and window boxes.
- Thin out annuals that were sown earlier, retaining the best and strongest plants.
- Pull up spring bedding plants, such as wallflowers and forget-me-nots, and add to compost pile. Sow seeds of these biennials now for next year.
- Lightly shear back early spring-flowering perennials, such as aubrietia, arabis, and perennial alyssum.
- Plant out dahlia tubers, making sure to drive in the stakes first, to avoid damage to tubers.

Trees, shrubs and climbers

- Check for aphids on roses, and either rub off or apply an insecticidal soap.
- Train or tie in young shoots of climbers to cover desired space evenly. After flowering, reduce some of the tangled growth of *Clematis montana* if space is restricted.
- Prune deciduous shrubs after flowering.
- Remove seed heads from rhododendrons and azaleas. Mulch them lightly at the extremity of the rootball (not on top of the rootball) with well-rotted compost. This will help to retain moisture and protect roots from drying out. Do this also for other shallow-rooted evergreens, such as camellias.

Fruits, vegetables and herbs

- Continue successive sowings of lettuce, carrots, spinach, radishes, bush beans, pole beans, and potatoes.
- Start winter crops of cauliflower, broccoli, Brussels sprouts, cabbages and pumpkins. Start main crop of potatoes. Plant asparagus.
- Feed tomato plants, remove side shoots, and plant out after the fifteenth of the month. Also plant out peppers, eggplants and squashes, including zucchini.
- Sow corn, cucumber and squash at the end of the month. Plant corn in blocks for better pollination.
- Take cuttings of rosemary, sage and thyme.

Other garden activities

- Keep newly turfed or sown lawns well watered.
- Continue preparing new lawns and repairing worn patches on existing ones.

What to Do

Done

May Garden Highlights

Bulbs

Allium spp. (ornamental onions), *Anemone blanda* (windflower), *Convallaria majilis* (lily-of-the-valley)*, *Endymion hispanicus* (Spanish bluebell), *Leucojum aestivum* (summer snowflake), *Muscari* spp. (grape hyacinth)*, *Narcissus* spp. (daffodils and narcissus)*, *Ornithogalum umbellatum* (star of Bethlehem).

Perennials

Aquilegia spp. (columbine), *Armeria maritima* (thrift), *Astrantia* spp. (masterwort), *Brunnera macrophylla*, *Centaurea montana* (mountain bluet), *Centranthus ruber* (valerian), *Delphinium* hybrids, *Dianthus* spp. (pinks)*, *Euphorbia* spp. (spurge), *Gentian acaulis* (gentian), *Geranium* spp. (hardy geranium), *Geum* spp., *Helianthemum* spp. (sun rose, rock rose), *Heuchera* spp. (coral bells), *Hosta*, *Iberis sempervirens* (candytuft), *Lupinus* spp. (lupine), *Meconopsis* spp. (blue poppy), *Paeonia* spp. (peony)*, *Papaver* spp. (poppy), *Saxifraga* × *urbium* (London pride), *Stachys byzantina* (woolly lamb's ears), *Trillium* spp.

Climbers

Clematis alpina, *C. macropetela*, *C. montana**, *Wisteria* spp.*

Shrubs

Ceanothus (California lilac), *Choisya ternata* (Mexican orange)*, *Cistus* spp. (rockrose), *Deutzia* spp., *Kalmia latifolia* (mountain laurel), *Kolkwitzia amabilis* (beauty bush), *Rhododendron* spp. and hybrids (rhododendrons and azaleas), *Rosa* spp. (rose)*, *Spiraea thunbergii* (spirea), *S.* × *vanhouttei*, *Syringa* spp. (lilac)*, *Viburnum plicatum*, *V. opulus*, *Weigela* spp.

Trees

Aesculus hippocastanum (horse chestnut), *Cornus nuttallii* (western white dogwood), *C. florida*, *Crataegus* spp. (hawthorn)*, *Gleditsia triacanthos* (honey locust), *Laburnum* (golden chain tree), *Magnolia sieboldii**, *Malus* spp. (crab apples).

* indicates fragrance

What's in Bloom   Week   1   2   3   4

Thoughts for Next Year

Design Ideas

Garden Notes

Week 1

Week 2

Garden Notes

Week 3

Week 4

Garden Images

Forget-me-nots

Gardening events, guest speakers, television and radio gardening programs, book and magazine references, horticultural information phone lines, gardening courses, etc.

Gardening Tips

Building a cold frame

Cold frames are extremely useful year-round for gardeners who are growing plants from cuttings or from seed. They protect seedlings and young plants from extreme weather conditions, yet provide them with cool nights and warm daytime temperatures. They can also be used to overwinter plants that are not reliably hardy outdoors. While there are now a number of lightweight cold frames on the market, with some that can even be folded up and put away after use, it is easy to build your own.

Method

An inexpensive and simple cold frame can be made by building a bottomless wooden box, with a base of sand or gravel to provide good drainage for pots and flats. Make the frame of the box higher at the back than the front so that the lid will be sloping when closed, with the slope facing south.

The lid can be an old window or piece of heavy-gauge plastic tacked on to a wood frame and attached to the back of the box with hinges. The hinges allow the lid to be propped open when it becomes too hot inside. An inexpensive thermometer hung inside will tell you when this is necessary.

When the temperature falls, cover the cold frame with blankets or evergreen branches to prevent frost from killing the young seedlings.

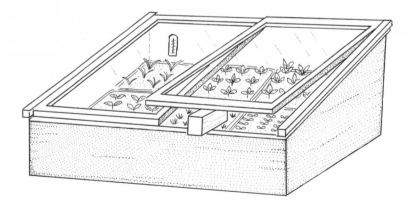

June

❈ All the hard work of the spring pays off in June. This is the time to potter and tidy in the garden, weed and water as necessary, and enjoy the blooms of roses, perennials and summer shrubs from the comfort of a garden chair. An important, and often overlooked, feature of an attractive garden is the appearance of the lawn. This month's gardening tips will help you keep a healthy, chemical-free lawn, simply by following a regular care and maintenance program. ❈ One of the lesser-known native North American bulbs is the striking camassia, which flowers from April to June. In some areas of the Pacific Northwest, camassias bloom in great abundance. They grow in moist meadows or marshes, where their lovely blue, white or purple flower spikes and star-shaped flowers add a splash of colour to the surrounding green. ❈ Camassias are from 2 to 3 feet (60 to 90 cm) tall, with one flowering stem and narrow, pointed, mid-green leaves. Perhaps the best known in our area is *Camassia quamash,* with loose clusters of bluish-purple flowers; *C. cusikii* has dense clusters of pale-blue star-shaped flowers; and *C. leichtlinii* has large clusters of creamy-white flowers.

June Check List

Annuals, perennials and bulbs
- Keep planting out bedding plants. Feed regularly with organic fertilizer and water well. Keep an eye on containers and hanging baskets, as they dry out quickly.
- Keep watering bulbs until leaves have turned yellow and can be gently removed.
- Continue staking tall perennials, and keep perennial beds neat by picking fresh flowers for indoor display and faded flowers for the compost.
- Divide up German bearded irises after flowering.
- Sow perennials, such as phlox, yarrow, columbine, lupine and delphinium, in a seed bed for next summer.
- Mulch lilies with compost or well-rotted manure.

Trees, shrubs and climbers
- Prune back deciduous shrubs, such as mock orange, after flowering.
- Start taking shrub cuttings.
- Cut back suckers on lilacs, and prune off faded flower heads.
- Deadhead rhododendrons and azaleas, and mulch if not already done.
- Keep newly planted hedges, trees, and shrubs well watered.
- Check for aphids, mildew, and black spot on roses, and pick off and destroy diseased leaves.

Fruits, vegetables and herbs
- Remove about one-third of the immature apples to get bigger fruit and prevent branches breaking from too much weight later on.
- Plant out tomatoes, zucchini and cucumbers.
- Thin out earlier sowings and continue to sow lettuce, carrots, spinach and radishes.
- Keep vegetable garden well weeded and watch for signs of pests and diseases.
- Continue to nip out side shoots of single-stemmed varieties of tomatoes, and support with stakes.
- Continue sowing winter vegetables. Start rutabagas and late cold crops.
- Cut off flowers of chives to encourage new foliage.

Other garden activities
- Finish all pool planting.
- Mow lawn regularly, keeping it at least 2 inches (5 cm) high, and keep well watered.
- Turn compost.
- Maintain a regular check for disease and insect problems.
- Feed house plants and move outside into a shady spot for their annual summer holiday.

What to Do

Done

June Garden Highlights

Bulbs

Allium spp. (ornamental onions), *Camassia* (camas), *Eremurus robustus* (foxtail lily), *Lilium candidum* (Madonna lily)*, *L. regale* (lily)*.

Perennials

Achillea (yarrow), *Aconitum* spp. (monkshood), *Alchemilla mollis* (Lady's mantle), *Aruncus dioicus* (goatsbeard), *Astilbe,. Campanula* spp. (bellflowers), *Delphinium* hybrids, *Dictamnus albus* (gas plant)*, *Digitalis* spp. (foxglove), *Filipendula* spp. (meadowsweet), *Hemerocallis* spp. (daylily)*, *Iris sibirica* (iris), *I. versicolor* (iris), *Lychnis* spp., *Papaver* spp. (poppy), *Paeonia* spp. (peony)*, *Phlomis* spp. (Jerusalem sage), *Polemonium caeruleum* (Jacob's ladder), *Thalictrum* spp. (meadow rue), *Tradescantia* spp. (spiderwort), *Trollius* spp. (globeflower), *Verbascum* spp. (mullein), *Zantedeschia aethiopica* (calla lily).

Climbers

Hydrangea anomala ssp. *petiolaris* (climbing hydrangea), *Lonicera* spp. (honeysuckle)*, *Rosa* spp. (climbing and rambling roses)*, *Solanum crispum* (potato vine).

Shrubs

Buddleia alternifolia (butterfly bush), *Kolkwitzia amabilis* (beauty bush), *Philadelphus* spp. (mock orange)*, *Potentilla* spp. (cinquefoil), *Rosa* spp. (roses)*, *Weigela*.

Trees

Cornus kousa (Japanese dogwood), *Robinia pseudoacacia* (black locust), *Styrax japonica* (Japanese snowbell tree)*.

* indicates fragrance

What's in Bloom

	Week	1	2	3	4

Thoughts for Next Year

Design Ideas

Garden Notes

Week 1

Week 2

Garden Notes

Week 3

Week 4

Garden Images

Forget-me-nots

Gardening events, guest speakers, television and radio gardening programs, book and magazine references, horticultural information phone lines, gardening courses, etc.

Gardening Tips

Taking care of the lawn

It is not necessary to use chemicals to have a good-looking lawn. With these simple strategies you can minimize maintenance and still feel proud of your lawn.

De-thatching: Some lawns have a dense layer of dead grass that forms into a thick mat and stops the penetration of water to grass roots. It is usually a result of poor drainage, overfertilization and overwatering. Routine raking may keep it in check, but a springtime or early fall scarification with a rented machine is better. The dead grass is brought to the surface and should be removed.

Aeration: Soil compaction is usually the greatest threat to lawns. Compressed particles in the topsoil reduce the movement of air, water, and nutrients to grass roots, causing stress to the grass and making it vulnerable to weeds, disease, moss and thatch build-up. It is worth aerating the soil twice a year, spring and fall, with a plug remover. Grass plugs may be left on the lawn or raked up.

Top-dressing: After aerating the lawn, top-dress with a layer of topsoil, sand or compost, or a mixture of loam, sand and organic matter. Successful lawns depend on a nutrient-rich, physically aerated, 6-inch (15-cm) layer of topsoil. Compost makes the best all-round soil conditioner. Sift it through a screen and spread the finer-grade material anytime throughout the growing season, especially after aerating.

Liming the soil: In our rainy climate, salts leach quickly out of the soil, leaving it too acidic for healthy grass. Spring and fall dusting with dolomite lime will re-balance the soil. Distribute an even dusting over the lawn surface, using a spreader set to appropriate density, as per directions.

Seeding: Bare patches should be reseeded with seed mixes appropriate to your area and available from your garden store. Plant new lawn in late summer or early fall, when warm days, light rains and cool nights provide the best growing conditions. Roots will be well established to provide a healthy lawn for the following year.

Mowing: Grass is much healthier if it is left a bit long. Longer grass shades any bare patches, making it difficult for weed seeds to germinate, and causes less stress to grass plants. Keep your mower blades sharp and as high as possible (about 3 inches/7 cm) and allow it to grow about an inch (2.5 cm) before cutting it again. Grass clippings can be left on the lawn.

Watering: Water long enough to give the lawn a deep soaking to the roots, to a depth of 4 to 6 inches (10 to 15 cm). Deep roots aid survival through dry summers. Frequent, shallow waterings simply encourage the roots to grow at a shallow level, and do more harm than good.

Of course, you may still feel that grass is too much work. Attractive green alternatives include a moss or thyme lawn or a wildflower meadow.

July

✿ In July, fruit, herb and vegetable gardens begin to yield in abundance. Strawberries and raspberries, sweet basil and thyme, and the first garden tomatoes and zucchini are all ready for harvest. July is also the time to take cuttings of tender perennials, such as geraniums (*Pelargonium* spp.), so that new plants will be well established inside before winter comes. (See this month's gardening tips.) ✿ Although roses, the featured plant this month, are usually associated with June and midsummer, it is the everbearing hybrid teas, floribundas and modern shrub roses that provide continuity and colour in the garden during July, August and September, often blooming bravely right into October. ✿ Perhaps the most romantic of all the flowers, the rose has been given for centuries as an expression of love and affection. How lucky we are to be able to grow such a wide variety, from the elegant, single-flowered species to the fragrantly extravagant blooms of damask and cabbage roses. Roses can be grown as shrubs, climbers and hedges, in containers and as ground cover. They can be used to soften arbours, trellises and walls, and are equally at home in a formal rose garden and a mixed border.

July Check List

Annuals, perennials and bulbs

- Water flowers in containers and hanging baskets daily.
- Regularly deadhead annuals and perennials to encourage flowering.
- When delphiniums fade, cut to ground level to stimulate second bloom.
- Make sure tall plants have support.
- Lift bearded irises after flowering, divide and replant.
- Pinch back chrysanthemums and asters to promote bushiness.
- Dry flowers for winter decoration.
- Plant autumn bulbs such as colchicum and autumn crocus.
- Take geranium (*Pelargonium* spp.) cuttings.

Trees, shrubs and climbers

- Prune deciduous shrubs, such as weigela, mock orange, and deutzia, after flowering.
- Give hedges a light pruning to keep them tidy.
- Deadhead roses and water well. Feed with rose food.
- Take cuttings of hebe, senecio and lavender.

Fruits, vegetables and herbs

- Harvest vegetables and continue sowings of lettuce, peas, kale, leeks, Swiss chard, broad beans, bush beans, beets, carrots, green onions and winter vegetables, such as winter cauliflower and purple sprouting broccoli.
- Continue feeding vegetables and water them regularly.
- Stop cutting rhubarb now, so that the plant can store energy. Keep it well watered.
- Harvest raspberries and strawberries. Remove unwanted strawberry runners and throw out plants that have cropped for three summers.
- Harvest bush fruits and cut out fruited canes.
- Cut herbs for freezing and drying.

General garden activities

- Mow lawn regularly and keep edges trimmed.
- Add waste from vegetable garden to compost. Keep it moist and turn regularly.
- Keep garden well watered.

What to Do

Done

July Garden Highlights

Bulbs

Allium spp. (ornamental onions), *Begonia, Camassia* (camas), *Cardiocrinum giganteum* (giant Himalayan lily)*, *Gladiolus* spp.*, *Lilium* spp. (lilies)*, *Tigridia* spp. (tiger flower).

Perennials

Acanthus spp. (bear's breeches), *Agapanthus africanus* (lily-of-the-Nile), *Alstroemeria* (Peruvian lily), *Campanula lactiflora* (bellflower), *Chrysanthemum* × *superbum* (shasta daisy), *Echinacea purpurea* (purple coneflower), *Echinops* spp. (globe thistle), *Eryngium* spp. (sea holly), *Gaillardia* × *grandiflora* (blanket flower), *Helenium autumnale* (sneezeweed), *Kniphofia* spp. (red hot poker), *Liatris* spp. (gay feather), *Lysimachia punctata* (yellow loosestrife), *Monarda didyma* (bergamot)*, *Nepeta mussinii* (catmint)*, *Penstemon* spp. (beard-tongue), *Phlox* spp.*, *Rodgersia, Rudbeckia* spp. (coneflower or black-eyed Susan), various ornamental grasses.

Climbers

Clematis hybrids, *Jasminum officinale* (poet's jasmine)*, *Lathyrus latifolius* (perennial sweet pea), *Passiflora* spp. (passion flower)*, *Rosa* hybrids (climbing roses)*.

Shrubs

Escallonia spp., *Fuchsia magellanica* (hardy fuchsia), *Hebe* spp., *Lavandula angustifolia* (lavender)*, *Rosa* hybrids (roses)*, *Senecio* 'Sunshine', *Spiraea* 'Anthony Waterer' (spirea), *Tamarix* spp. (tamarisk), *Yucca* spp.

Trees

Liriodendron tulipifera (tulip tree), *Magnolia grandiflora* (southern magnolia)*.

* indicates fragrance.

What's in Bloom

	Week	1	2	3	4

Thoughts for Next Year

Design Ideas

Garden Notes

Week 1

Week 2

Garden Notes

Week 3

Week 4

Garden Images

Forget-me-nots

Gardening events, guest speakers, television and radio gardening programs, book and magazine references, horticultural information phone lines, gardening courses, etc.

Gardening Tips

How to take and overwinter pelargonium cuttings

Taking pelargonium cuttings and overwintering them is satisfying and easy, and the best time to do this is from July to September.

Taking Cuttings

Choose a healthy shoot without flowers or flower buds. Using a sharp knife, cut the shoot off just below a node, so that the cutting is 3-4 inches long (8-10 cm). Remove the lower leaves but leave at least three leaves per cutting.

Fill 3-inch (7.5-cm) pots three-quarters full with potting mixture, and make a hole for the cutting with a pencil or a piece of dowel. Drop the cutting into the hole, press firmly in place, and add more mixture. Water it well and then keep it on the dry side, giving it a little water when necessary so that it does not wilt. During the winter months, water sparingly and keep in a cool light room.

Harden off in April or May, either by setting plants out during the day and bringing them in at night or by placing them in a cold frame. Plant out in the garden at the end of May.

Overwintering pelargonium plants

Dig up the plants in late September and shake off soil, being careful not to damage the roots.

Plant in fresh potting mixture in pots large enough to contain each plant's roots. Cut the stems down to half their height, removing all yellow leaves and dead flower heads.

Place the pots on a south-facing window ledge in an unheated room or in an unheated greenhouse. Water sparingly, and do not fertilize during the winter months.

In spring move the plants to a well-lit area and increase the amount of water. Harden them off in April, as above.

August

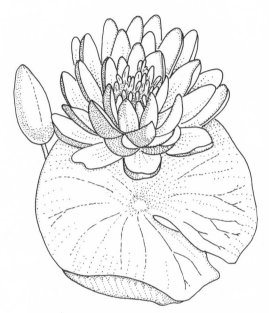

❈ In the heat of August, few things look as cool and inviting as a stretch of water, whether it is the ocean, the lake, a swimming pool or even a backyard water garden. Water gardens are increasingly popular. They provide endless hours of pleasure throughout the year and they are easy to keep and maintain (see this month's gardening tips).

❈ No water garden would be complete without a water lily or two. The *Nymphaea* spp. are surprisingly easy to grow, requiring only an adequate depth of water, some ordinary soil, and a sunny position. Water lilies bloom from the beginning of June throughout the summer, becoming dormant in the fall and reappearing the following spring. ❈ There are water lilies native to almost every continent. Most of the ones in cultivation today are hybrids, and there are many to choose from, with beautiful, cup-shaped, pink, white or yellow flowers. Some are suitable for large ponds or lakes, and some are ideal for small containers, such as half-barrels. Their large round or heart-shaped leaves provide shade for fish and help inhibit the growth of algae.

August Check List

Annuals, perennials and bulbs

- Water plants copiously and keep deadheading annuals and perennials.
- Dry flowers for winter decoration.
- Feed plants in tubs, window boxes and hanging baskets with fish fertilizer.
- Plant out perennial seedlings, such as delphiniums, and biennials, such as wallflowers, that were started earlier.
- Take cuttings of alpines, such as pinks (*Dianthus* spp.).
- Continue taking cuttings of garden geraniums (*Pelargonium* spp.).
- Collect seeds of plants you wish to propagate.
- Order peonies from catalogues to plant in the next few months.

Trees, shrubs and climbers

- Keep evergreens well mulched.
- Continue taking cuttings from shrubs such as camellia, escallonia, weigela and butterfly bush (*Buddleia davidii*).
- Prune back wisteria and other vigorous climbers to control vegetative growth.
- Keep deadheading roses and keep them well watered. Order roses for planting in late fall and winter.
- Finish pruning rambler roses.
- Clip lavender as flowers fade.
- Trim hedges.

Fruits, vegetables and herbs

- Harvest vegetables frequently and keep vegetable plants well watered.
- Keep sowing winter vegetables, lettuce, spinach, radishes, turnips and Chinese vegetables up to August 15.
- Cut raspberry canes that have finished fruiting to ground level, and tie new canes to supports.
- Continue to collect herbs for freezing and drying, and take cuttings of rosemary, lavender, oregano, rue and bay laurel.
- Summer-prune espaliered fruit trees.
- Remove the tops of single-stemmed tomato plants (not bush types) at the fourth truss and fertilize.

General garden activities

- Mow lawn regularly and prepare ground for sowing new lawns next month.
- Turn compost and keep moist.

What to Do

Done

August Garden Highlights

Bulbs

Acidanthera murieliae*, *Agapanthus africanus* (lily-of-the-Nile), *Crocosmia* spp. (montbretia), *Dahlia* spp. and hybrids (dahlias), *Galtonia* spp. (summer hyacinth)*, *Lilium* spp. (lilies)*.

Perennials

Althaea spp. (hollyhock), *Artemisia* spp. (wormwood), *Chrysanthemum* spp. (florists' chrysanthemum), *C. frutescens* (marguerite daisy), *Gypsophila paniculata* (baby's breath), *Heliopsis* spp. (oxeye daisy), *Hypericum calycinum* (St. John's wort), *Inula* spp. (elecampane), *Salvia superba* (salvia).

Climbers

Clematis spp. and hybrids, *Jasminum officinale* (jasmine)*, *Lonicera* spp. (honeysuckle), *Rosa* hybrids (climbing and rambling roses)*, *Tropaeolum speciosum* spp. (flame creeper).

Shrubs

Abelia × *grandiflora* (abelia), *Calluna vulgaris* (heather), *Caryopteris* × *clandonensis* (bluebeard)*, *Clethra alnifolia* (summersweet)*, *Hydrangea* spp. (hydrangea), *Rosa* spp. (roses).

Trees

Clerodendrum trichotomum (glorybower)*, *Magnolia grandiflora* (southern magnolia)*.

* indicates fragrance

What's in Bloom   Week 1   2   3   4

Thoughts for Next Year

Design Ideas

Garden Notes

Week 1

Week 2

Garden Notes

Week 3

Week 4

Garden Images

Forget-me-nots

Gardening events, guest speakers, television and radio gardening programs, book and magazine references, horticultural information phone lines, gardening courses, etc.

Gardening Tips

Maintaining a water garden

Once established, a water garden is relatively undemanding, for when a pond's plant and animal life is in balance, it becomes a self-sustaining ecosystem. However, there are some simple maintenance activities that may be necessary from time to time.

Plant care: Remove dead and yellowing foliage regularly to keep plants clean and healthy. Water lilies benefit from annual feeding at the beginning of the growing season. While fertilizer tablets are commercially available, it's easy to make your own by mixing coarse bone meal with clay, forming the mixture into pellets. Tuck the pellets down among the plants' roots.

If a water lily develops too many leaves and the flowers are small, the plant should be divided, usually every three or four years. Do this in late spring when new growth has started. Simply lift the large plant from its container and cut off the side branches, including a good part of the root stock with each cutting. Plant each cutting separately in heavy, loamy soil in a plastic bucket or pot, with well-rotted manure in the bottom for nourishment. Cover the soil surface with gravel or sand to prevent disturbance of the soil, and place the pot at the bottom of the pool.

Algae control: Sometimes the pond water will turn a thick green, like pea soup. This is caused by minute algae feeding on mineral salts in the water, and they will die out once there is a good balance between plant and animal life. To help restore balance, ensure that one-third of the surface of the pond is covered with floating plants and water lily pads, and there is one bunch of submerged oxygenating plants per 2 square feet (0.185 square m) of pond surface. Scoop out any thick surface filaments of slimy green algae, and remove any extremely invasive spreaders. Draining and refilling the pool will just prolong the trouble.

Wildlife: Fish, frogs and water snails are all useful additions to the pond because they eat mosquito larvae, clean up and help to keep the pond in balance. However, herons and raccoons can be a problem. A 6-inch (15-cm) fence of small canes linked with fishing line may deter the heron, and marginal plants can be planted on a shelf in the middle of the pond, out of reach of busy raccoon paws.

Preparing for winter: Hardy aquatic plants and hardy water lilies die down naturally and will survive the winter on the bottom of the pond, where it is less likely to freeze. More exotic tropical plants will need to be taken indoors for the winter.

Tidy up marginal plants after the first frost, and reduce them to about two-thirds of their height. However, don't cut them below water level; some of them have hollow stems and will rot. If you have overhanging trees, cover the pond with netting until all the leaves have fallen; as the leaves decay, they release toxic gases that will harm the fish. Bring small portable water gardens indoors; they are more vulnerable to damage from winter temperature fluctuations.

September

✪ By September, many plants that looked fresh and appealing a month ago are beginning to die back and look straggly. However, there are a wide variety of attractive fall-blooming plants, such as Japanese anemones and asters, to breathe new life and colour into tired flower beds. You may want to incorporate more fall-blooming plants into your garden, and garden centres often offer a good variety at this time of year. From September through into early November is also the time to sow hardy annual seeds, and some ideas for this are included in the gardening tips for this month. ✪ The hydrangeas are some of those valuable, late-summer bloomers that bridge the summer and fall seasons and are an excellent choice for the city garden. An attractive species is *Hydrangea paniculata*, a native of Japan and China. It is a very hardy shrub with arching, conical trusses of cream-coloured flowers and mid-green leaves. Its enormous flowering heads turn pink with age and, like all hydrangea blooms, dry well if they are cut when they are in full bloom, just before they turn brown. In this way, they can be enjoyed in dried flower arrangements throughout the winter months.

September Check List

Annuals, perennials and bulbs

- Keep deadheading annuals and perennials and save seed pods of flowers you wish to propagate.
- Divide perennials and plant new ones.
- Plant peonies this month and next.
- When leaves of gladioli turn brown, the corms can be lifted and sun-dried for ten days. Store in a cool, well-ventilated, frost-free place.
- Sow sweet peas, poppies and cornflowers now for early summer flowering.
- Plant out wallflowers and add lime to soil.
- Begin planting spring-flowering bulbs. Shop early for best selection. Pot up some for flowering indoors.
- Dry flowers, including hydrangeas, for winter arrangements.
- Continue taking geranium (*Pelargonium* spp.) cuttings, and fuchsia, heliotrope and marguerite cuttings.

Trees, shrubs and climbers

- Order new roses and prepare new rose beds for planting in November. Top-dress with sulphate of potash to harden growth in preparation for winter.
- Prune summer-flowering heathers.
- Give hedges a final light trim.
- Continue taking shrub cuttings.
- Prepare soil for planting trees and shrubs in winter.

Fruits, vegetables and herbs

- Keep harvesting fruits and vegetables. Pull up tomato plants by the end of the month. Unripened fruit will ripen indoors.
- Continue sowing winter vegetables, lettuce, spinach, Swiss chard, and kale, and thin out earlier sowings.
- Start taking cuttings of bush fruits.
- Order new fruit trees and bushes to plant in winter. Prepare site by digging in compost and manure.

General garden activities

- Plant new lawns and/or renovate old ones, sowing seed on bare patches.
- Rake lawn to keep free of leaves. Wire rake to get rid of thatch buildup and aerate if necessary.
- Remove yellowed leaves from water plants. Remove, clean and store water pump.

What to Do   Done

September Garden Highlights

Bulbs

Colchicum autumnale and *Crocus* spp.* (autumn crocus); *Crocosmia* spp. (montbretia); *Cyclamen hederifolium*, also called *C. neopolitanum* (hardy cyclamen); *Dahlia* spp.; *Freesia* × *hybrida* (freesia)*; *Leucojum autumnale* (autumn snowflake); *Nerine bowdenii* (nerine).

Perennials

Anaphalis spp. (pearly everlasting), *Anemone* × *hybrida* (Japanese anemone), *Aster* spp. (Michaelmas daisy), *Chrysanthemum* spp., *Liriope muscari* (lily turf), *Physalis alkekengi* (Chinese lantern), *Schizostylis coccinea* (Kaffir lily), *Sedum spectabile* (stonecrop), *Solidago* hybrids (goldenrod), *Stokesia laevis* (Stokes' aster).

Climbers

Clematis orientalis, *C. paniculata**, *C. tangutica*, *Polygonum aubertii* (fleece vine, silver lace vine).

Shrubs

Callicarpa bodinieri (beautyberry), *Calluna vulgaris* (heather), *Cotinus coggygria* (smoke bush), *Erica cineria* (scotch heath, bell heather), *Hydrangea paniculata* 'Grandiflora' (Peegee hydrangea), *Spartium junceum* (Spanish broom)*.

Trees

Magnolia grandiflora (southern magnolia)*.

* indicates fragrance

What's in Bloom

	Week	1	2	3	4

Thoughts for Next Year

Design Ideas

Garden Notes

Week 1

Week 2

Garden Notes

Week 3

Week 4

Garden Images

Forget-me-nots

Gardening events, guest speakers, television and radio gardening programs, book and magazine references, horticultural information phone lines, gardening courses, etc.

Gardening Tips

Hardy annuals to sow in the fall

Hardy annuals germinate at low temperatures and can withstand light frost. The hardiest of these can be sown directly in the garden this month and will germinate and survive the winter as seedlings. These fall-sown annuals bloom earlier than those sown in the spring, and their flowers are bigger and stronger. Good ones to try include *Centaurea cyanus* (cornflower, bachelor's button), *Clarkia amoena* (godetia, farewell to spring), *Eschscholzia californica* (California poppy), *Lathyrus odoratus* (sweet pea), *Linum grandiflorum* and *L. usitatissimum* (flowering flax and common flax), *Nigella damascena* (love-in-a-mist), *Papaver* spp. (poppy), and *Rudbeckia hirta* (gloriosa daisy).

Method

Turn the soil with a spading fork to one fork's depth, removing stones and breaking up lumps. Cover the soil with 2 or 3 inches (5 to 7.5 cm) of compost or well-rotted manure and mix the soil and compost with the spading fork. Rake over the seed bed several times.

Mark off the area you wish to sow. One simple method is to use a grid. With a hoe handle, press grid lines into the soil. Separate the grid lines by the planting distance specified on the seed package. For example, if the mature plants need 6 inches (15 cm) between them, the grid lines should be 6 inches (15 cm) apart. Sow the seeds at the point where the lines intersect. This method makes it easy to distinguish between weeds and the young plants.

If seeds are very small, mix them first with fine sand to make them easier to distribute, and sprinkle the mixture on the prepared soil. They do not need covering, but all other seeds should be sown slightly deeper than recommended on the seed package, since they are being sown just before winter.

After the seeds are sown, press the soil down firmly, and water the area gently, keeping the soil moist until the seeds germinate.

Weed the seeded area by hand so that the young seedlings are not damaged. They can be thinned out now, but the final thinning should be done in February.

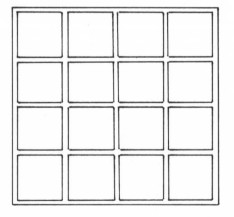

October

✿ October is an important month for moving and planting trees and shrubs; days and nights are cool and usually damp, and plants can be well settled into the ground before winter begins. Now is the time to move that purple rhododendron that you tagged in April, for instance, and introduce new plants; most garden centres will have a wide selection of trees and shrubs from which to choose. This is also a great time to get to know your neighbours and organize a neighbourhood project: banding trees to protect them from the destructive winter moth. (See this month's gardening tips.) ✿ A lovely native tree to add to a small garden is *Acer circinatum*, which has gnarled and twisted stems that resemble vines, hence its common name, vine maple. The tree has distinctive, rounded leaves, with seven- to nine-pointed lobes, and they turn red and orange in the fall, producing a brilliant, multi-coloured display. The stems are covered with young, red twigs, and the fruits are also reddish, differing from other maples in that the wings are set at right-angles to the stem. The tree bears clusters of tiny, 1/2-inch (1-cm) flowers in April, with reddish-purple sepals and white petals.

October Check List

Annuals, perennials and bulbs

- Continue planting spring-flowering bulbs and perennials.
- As perennials fade, lift and divide now, or label those you want to move or divide in the spring.
- Clear beds of annuals by the end of the month and add to compost.
- Dig up dahlias, gladioli and tuberous begonias; label and store in frost-free place.
- Cut stems of perennials, clean up borders and keep well weeded. Mulch with well-rotted compost or manure.
- Plant out wallflowers and forget-me-nots that were sown earlier.
- Plant lily bulbs from now until March.

Trees, shrubs and climbers

- Put sticky bands of Tanglefoot around trees to trap winter months.
- Good time to plant shrubs and trees.
- Lightly prune roses. Collect and destroy old leaves. Prune ramblers now, cutting old flowering stems down to ground level.
- Feed lilacs and other shrubs that are heavy feeders with bone meal.

Fruits, vegetables and herbs

- Keep harvesting fruits and vegetables, and make final sowing of lettuce in beds or the cold frame.
- Continue taking cuttings of bush fruits, prune back fruited canes, and stake the new ones.
- Take final cuttings of herbs, such as lavender, rosemary and bay laurel. Keep the cuttings indoors for the winter. Bay laurel should always be brought in for the winter, since it may not survive outside.
- Divide clumps of chives, and pot up young plants of mint, chives and parsley for indoor use.
- Cultivate and enrich soil in area you plan to sow in spring.
- Plant garlic, shallots and overwintering onions.

General garden activities

- Keep lawn free of leaves, and continue cutting it as long as it grows. Aerate and scarify if needed or not already done.
- Continue sowing new lawns.
- As leaves fall, put net over the pond and clean up pool for winter. Continue to feed fish as long as they are active. Lower pots of lilies to the bottom of the pond, cut back oxygenators and discard top growth.

What to Do

Done

October Garden Highlights

Bulbs

Colchicum autumnale and *Crocus* spp. (autumn crocus), *Cyclamen hederifolium* (hardy cyclamen), *Dahlia* spp., *Nerine bowdenii* (nerine).

Perennials

Anemone × *hybrida* (Japanese anemone), *Aster* spp. (Michaelmas daisy), *Chrysanthemum* spp., *Cortaderia selloana* (pampas grass), *Liriope muscari* (lily turf), *Schizostylis coccinea* (Kaffir lily), *Sedum spectabile* (stonecrop).

Climbers

Clematis orientalis, *C. tangutica*, *Parthenocissus quinquefolia* (Virginia creeper), *Vitis* spp. (grape vines).

Shrubs

Aucuba spp., *Berberis* spp. (barberry), *Cotinus coggygria* (smoke bush), *Cotoneaster* spp., *Euonymus europaeus* (spindle tree), *Fothergilla major*, *Hippophae rhamnoides* (sea buckthorn), *Pyracantha* spp. (firethorn), *Rosa moyesii* and *R. rugosa* (rose), *Skimmia* spp., *Symphoricarpos* spp. (snowberry), *Viburnum carlesii*, *V. opulus* (viburnum).

Trees

Acer spp. (maple), *Crataegus* spp. (hawthorn), *Hamamelis* spp. (witch hazel), *Liriodendron tulipifera* (tulip tree), *Rhus typhina* (stag's horn sumac), *Sorbus* spp. (mountain ash).

What's in Bloom   Week | 1 | 2 | 3 | 4

Thoughts for Next Year

Design Ideas

Garden Notes

Week 1

Week 2

Garden Notes

Week 3

Week 4

Garden Images

Forget-me-nots

Gardening events, guest speakers, television and radio gardening programs, book and magazine references, horticultural information phone lines, gardening courses, etc.

Gardening Tips

Control of the winter moth

The winter moth has become a major problem in some areas of the West Coast. The caterpillars attack a wide variety of trees and shrubs in March and early April. (See March gardening tips.) In October, when the wingless female moth climbs trees and shrubs to lay her eggs, we can interrupt the life cycle in an environmentally safe way.

Method

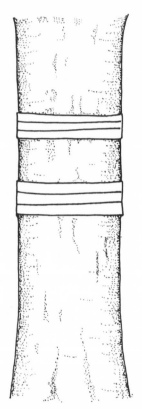

In late September or early October, apply two 6-inch-wide (15-cm) bands of masking tape (2-inch/5-cm-wide tape wrapped around the tree several times) around the tree trunk. Place the bands at about chest height — approximately 4 and 5 feet (120 and 150 cm) above ground level. Cover the bands with something sticky, such as Tanglefoot. The female moth will become trapped on the sticky substance as it climbs up the trunk. Make sure there are no gaps under the bands for the moth to crawl through.

The lower band should be replaced when it becomes covered with dead moths, or when moths begin to be trapped on the upper band. Bands should be removed and destroyed the following spring.

As this moth has few native predators, it is important to take measures to control the pest. Many of the eggs are laid in city-owned street trees, and the banding of trees can become a neighbourhood project.

November

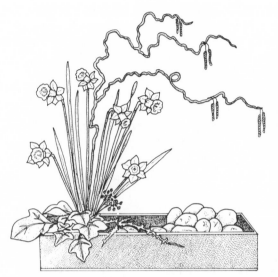

❁ This is the last chance for fall clean-up, and it is especially important to remove any pests and diseased foliage so that they don't overwinter in your garden. Although the weather in November may be dreary and wet, there are usually some days when it is possible to weed, plant and sow. This is the month when bare-root roses arrive, and the gardening tips for this month should help you to get them off to a healthy start. ❁ For most of the summer, the corkscrew hazel, *Corylus avellana* 'Contorta', is an unattractive mass of misshapen leaves. It is at its best in winter, when its curiously twisted branches have shed their leaves and are decorated instead with showy yellow catkins. The extraordinary shapes of its contorted branches make this hardy deciduous shrub a favourite of flower arrangers and a valuable addition to the garden. One cautionary note: it forms a dense, twiggy shrub 8 feet (2.7 m) tall, and equally wide, and thus needs plenty of room in the garden. It provides an excellent framework for one of the small-flowered clematis, such as a *C. viticella* or *C. texensis* cultivar, which will grow through the branches of the shrub in summer and die back in winter.

November Check List

Annuals, perennials and bulbs

- Complete bulb planting.
- Dig up dahlias and other summer bulbs if not already done.
- Clean up beds and borders and mulch with compost or manure.
- Make sure cushion plants like dianthus and saxifrage don't get covered in leaves, as they will rot.
- Write for seed catalogues.
- Cut back chrysanthemums when they have finished flowering.
- Pot up geraniums (*Pelargonium* spp.) and fuchsia and store in frost-free place. Water once a month.
- Continue to edge and weed flower beds.
- Continue sowing hardy annuals, such as poppies and cornflowers, and biennials, such as foxgloves.

Trees, shrubs and climbers

- Plant bare-root roses as they become available.
- Give roses a final deadheading and a light pruning. Apply some dolomite lime around established roses.
- Prune back newly planted and transplanted trees and shrubs to compensate for root loss.

Fruits, vegetables and herbs

- Plant new berry bushes and fruit trees.
- Continue taking cuttings of bush fruits and prune to remove crossed and crowded branches.
- Dig soil in vegetable garden as areas become vacant in preparation for planting early in the year. Add manure or compost to soil.
- Plant garlic, shallots and overwintering onions.

General garden activities

- Build or repair existing garden structures (fences, arbours, trellises).
- Sharpen and oil tools and service the lawn mower.
- This is a good time of year to have your soil tested and make improvements before spring planting.
- Spread dolomite lime around lime lovers, such as lilac, and over the vegetable garden (excluding the potato patch).
- Replan the vegetable garden for next year to allow for crop rotation.

What to Do

Done

November Garden Highlights

Bulbs

Cyclamen hederifolium, also called *C. neopolitanum* (hardy cyclamen), *Nerine bowdenii* (nerine).

Perennials

Iris unguicularis (Algerian iris)*, *Gentiana sino-ornata* (gentian), *Liriope muscarii* (lily turf), *Schizostylis coccinea* (Kaffir lily), *Serratula coccinea* (knapweed).

Climbers

Jasminum nudiflorum (winter jasmine).

Shrubs

Cornus alba 'Elegantissima' (Tatarian dogwood), *C. a.* 'Sibirica' (Siberian dogwood), *C. sericea* 'Flaviramea', also known as *C. stolonifera* 'Flaviramea' (red-osier dogwood).
   Also see October list.

Trees

Acer griseum (paperbark maple), *Prunus serrulata* (Japanese flowering cherry).
   Also see October list.

* indicates fragrance

What's in Bloom

Week	1	2	3	4

Thoughts for Next Year

Design Ideas

Garden Notes

Week 1

Week 2

Garden Notes

Week 3

Week 4

Garden Images

Forget-me-nots

Gardening events, guest speakers, television and radio gardening programs, book and magazine references, horticultural information phone lines, gardening courses, etc.

Gardening Tips

Success with bare-root roses

So many different kinds of roses are now available that it is possible your local nursery does not have the very rose you want.

Fortunately, there are many excellent specialist mail-order companies that supply bare-root roses. These roses are lifted from the ground at the nursery during the dormant season, from October to March, and shipped fresh, all soil removed from their roots, directly to the customer.

Selecting roses: Summer is the best time to make your selection. Browse through the rose books and catalogues, look at roses in parks, nurseries and private gardens, and make your choices. Roses are ordered in summer for fall delivery.

On arrival: Unpack the roses immediately and check them carefully. Remove any damaged shoots by cutting back to the first healthy bud below the damage. Cut out any decayed or thin shoots and remove leaves or hips. At the same time, cut back any damaged or long roots to 12 inches (30 cm). Cut out any suckers growing from the roots. Submerge them in a bucket of water for a couple of hours.

Preparing the planting mixture: A good planting mixture is important to get the roses off to a good start. Mix one part peat moss, one part mushroom manure and one part soil. Add to this a small handful of bone meal and mix well. One bucketful of this mixture per rose should be sufficient.

Preparing the ground: Dig the planting hole, making sure it is deep enough for the budding union (the point where the plant is budded onto the rootstock), which should be buried about 1 inch (2.5 cm) below soil level. The hole should also be wide enough for the roots to fan out as evenly as possible. Some roses have all their roots pointing in one direction, and these should be placed at one side of the planting hole so that they can grow naturally.

Planting: Hold the rose in position and cover the roots carefully with the planting mixture, firming the soil around the roots with careful treading. Add more planting mixture until the hole is full. Gently firm it again, ensuring that the bud union is in the right place. Water well and firm it once more.

Heeling in: Sometimes it is not possible or convenient to put roses into their permanent home right away. In this case, dig a hole or trench about 12 inches (30 cm) deep and large enough to accommodate the roots; place the roses in the trench about 3 to 6 inches (7 to 15 cm) apart, at an angle of 45 degrees. Replace the soil and firm down, making sure that the budding union is 2 inches (5 cm) below the ground. Water well. The roses can be left heeled in like this for a month or two, if necessary.

December

❃ As the year draws to a close, it's time to take stock of your achievements in the garden and look forward to a new season. You'll want to order seed and plant catalogues, and look for presents for your gardening friends and relatives. You might want to consider giving a plant that can also be enjoyed by the birds and butterflies that visit the garden every year. There is a wide variety of fruit-bearing and berry trees and shrubs that will attract them, especially native species, and the list in the gardening tips for this month will give you some ideas. ❃ One of the few perennials that flower in the middle of winter is the Christmas rose, *Helleborus niger*. Although it is associated by name with Christmas, it usually flowers in January and February. It has dark-green, deeply-lobed evergreen leaves and delicate, saucer-shaped white "flowers" (actually petal-like sepals) that rise directly from the ground on 9- to 12-inch (22-to 30-cm) stems. The lovely, translucent sepals, with gold stamens in the centre, illuminate the winter garden. The long-lasting flowers are produced intermittently from late December to early March.

December Check List

Annuals, perennials and bulbs

- Protect crowns of tender plants on frosty nights.
- Divide and replant perennials, weather permitting, and firm down plants whose roots are loosened by frost.
- Start ordering flower seeds.
- Check dahlia and begonia tubers, and gladioli corms, and remove infected ones.

Trees, shrubs and climbers

- Trees and shrubs may be planted, weather permitting.
- Lightly prune hollies and evergreens, and use clippings for wreaths and seasonal decorations.
- Continue to plant roses if ground is not frozen or waterlogged.
- Rake up and destroy old rose leaves to prevent overwintering of diseases.

Fruits, vegetables and herbs

- Plant fruit trees and bushes in good weather.
- Mulch herb bushes if weather turns severe.
- Plan vegetable garden and start ordering seeds.
- Begin spraying fruit trees with dormant oil and lime sulphur in mild weather.
- Check stored fruit and other produce and remove any that are rotting.
- Ventilate cold frames in mild weather.

General garden activities

- Rake leaves and debris off lawns and avoid walking on frozen grass.
- Take the opportunity to clean and sharpen tools and service the mower and any other power equipment.

What to Do

Done

December Garden Highlights

Bulbs

Crocus, early species, *Cyclamen coum* (cyclamen), *Galanthus nivalis* (snowdrop).

Perennials

Helleborus niger (Christmas rose), *Iris unguicularis* (Algerian iris)*.

Climbers

Jasminum nudiflorum (winter jasmine).

Shrubs

Camellia sasanqua, *Cornus* spp. (see October), *Daphne mezereum* (February daphne)*, *Erica* spp. (heath), *Fatsia japonica* (Japanese aralia), *Ilex* spp. (holly), *Mahonia* 'Charity'*, *Viburnum* × *bodnantense*, *Viburnum tinus* (laurustinus).

Trees

Prunus subhirtella 'Autumnalis' (autumn-flowering cherry). See also Garden Highlights for November.

* indicates fragrance

What's in Bloom

	Week	1	2	3	4

Thoughts for Next Year

Design Ideas

Garden Notes

Week 1

Week 2

Garden Notes

Week 3

Week 4

Garden Images

Forget-me-nots

Gardening events, guest speakers, television and radio gardening programs, book and magazine references, horticultural information phone lines, gardening courses, etc.

Gardening Tips

Attracting birds and butterflies to your garden

There's a great advantage to keeping areas of your garden "wild and natural." The more comfortable the habitat is for birds and butterflies, the more likely you are to attract an interesting variety of them. As you learn more about the habits and needs of various species, you can include more of the plants, nesting spots and habitats they like, and their numbers will increase in your garden.

Birds

Birds like water, especially the sound of dripping or moving water, so it helps to have a permanent water feature, such as a fountain, birth bath or pond. To attract birds, include native plants; they are hardy, easy to grow, familiar to the birds and provide food suitable for them. This includes blueberries, blackberries, huckleberries and salmonberries, and shrubs such as Oregon grape (*Mahonia aquifolium*), elderberry (*Sambucus* spp.), salal (*Gaultheria shallon*), Saskatoon berry (*Amelanchier* spp.), red-osier dogwood (*Cornus stolonifera*), hazelnut (*Corylus cornuta*), sumac (*Rhus glabra*), red-flowering currant (*Ribes sanguineum*), wild rose (*Rosa* spp.), and snowberry (*Symphoricarpos albus*). Other bushes attractive to birds include *Cotoneaster* spp., *Pyracantha* spp., cultivated honeysuckles (*Lonicera* spp.), *Viburnum* spp. and cultivated berry bushes. Fruit-producing trees to grow include mountain ash (*Sorbus sitchensis*), the dogwoods (*Cornus* spp.), hawthorn (*Crataegus* spp.), and crab apple (*Malus* spp.). Conifers such as fir, juniper and pine offer year-round cover and seeds for food.

Hummingbirds and butterflies

Many trumpet-shaped flowers are designed to be pollinated by creatures with long, sucking mouthparts, like the proboscis of a butterfly or the long, hollow, pointed bill of a hummingbird. Hummingbirds are especially attracted to red and orange, butterflies to purple and yellow.

Native plants that attract hummingbirds and butterflies could include bog rosemary (*Andromeda polifolia*), kinnikinnick (*Arctostaphylos uva-ursi*), columbine (*Aquilegia* spp.), salal (*Gaultheria shallon*), fireweed (*Epilobium angustifolium*), western trumpet honeysuckle (*Lonicera ciliosa*), *Penstemon* spp., red-flowering currant (*Ribes sanguineum*), salmonberry (*Rubus spectabilis*), tiger lily (*Lilium columbianum*), foxglove (*Digitalis* spp.) and huckleberry. Other ornamental nectar-source plants include horse chestnut (*Aesculus* spp.), locust (*Robinia* spp.), *Weigela* spp., flowering quince (*Chaenomeles* spp.), *Daphne* spp., heathers (*Erica* spp.), *Pieris japonica*, trumpet vine (*Campsis radicans*), *Fuschia* spp., *Primula* spp., lilac (*Syringa* spp.), chives (*Allium),* pinks and carnations (*Dianthus* spp.), red valerian (*Centranthus ruber*), butterfly bush (*Buddleia*), yarrow (*Achillea millefolium*), *Phlox* spp., nasturtium (*Tropaeolum majus*), *Petunia* spp., *Gladiolus* spp., *Delphinium* spp., blackberries, scarlet runner beans and Michaelmas daisies.

Foods for developing young butterfly larvae

To attract butterflies, you will need to consider the needs of caterpillars as well. Not surprisingly, native plants are best. They include common "weeds," such as stinging nettles (*Urtica dioica*), bull thistle (*Circium vulgare*), and Queen Anne's lace (*Caucus carota*). Trees that feed larvae include arbutus, birch, poplar and willow. Meadow grasses are important too, as are the milkweeds (*Asclepias* spp.) and pearly everlasting (*Anaphalis margaritacea*).

Plant Wish List

Name	Comments	Where to plant

Friendship Garden Plants

Plant	Received from	Where located

Plant	Promised to	Comments

Vegetables and herbs

Plant	Sowing/planting Date	Harvesting Date	Yield, Flavour, Comments

Propagation Record

Plant	Date started	Date rooted or germinated	Date moved outdoors

Pruning Record

What	When	How

Pest and Disease Control

Date	Problem	Remedy and Results

Mistakes to Avoid

Mistake	Comments

Plants, Bulbs, Seeds

Name	Supplier	Date ordered	Date received	Comments

Garden and Lawn Service Contracts

Company	Services rendered	Cost	Comments

Clubs and Magazines

Subscription	Amount	Date Paid

Gardening Book Wish List

Title	Author	Cost

Gardens Visited: Public and Private

Date	Name and Location	Plants of Interest	Comments

Nurseries and Garden Centres

Name ....
Address ....
....
.... Tel. No. ....
Specialty ....
....

Name ....
Address ....
....
.... Tel. No. ....
Specialty ....
....

Name ....
Address ....
....
.... Tel. No. ....
Specialty ....
....

Name ....
Address ....
....
.... Tel. No. ....
Specialty ....
....

Name ....
Address ....
....
.... Tel. No. ....
Specialty ....
....

Name ....
Address ....
....
.... Tel. No. ....
Specialty ....
....

Name ....
Address ....
....
.... Tel. No. ....
Specialty ....
....

Name ....
Address ....
....
.... Tel. No. ....
Specialty ....
....

Name ....
Address ....
....
.... Tel. No. ....
Specialty ....
....

Name ....
Address ....
....
.... Tel. No. ....
Specialty ....
....

Nurseries and Garden Centres

Name ....
Address ....
....
.... Tel. No. ....
Specialty ....
....

Name ....
Address ....
....
.... Tel. No. ....
Specialty ....
....

Name ....
Address ....
....
.... Tel. No. ....
Specialty ....
....

Name ....
Address ....
....
.... Tel. No. ....
Specialty ....
....

Name ....
Address ....
....
.... Tel. No. ....
Specialty ....
....

Name ....
Address ....
....
.... Tel. No. ....
Specialty ....
....

Name ....
Address ....
....
.... Tel. No. ....
Specialty ....
....

Name ....
Address ....
....
.... Tel. No. ....
Specialty ....
....

Name ....
Address ....
....
.... Tel. No. ....
Specialty ....
....

Name ....
Address ....
....
.... Tel. No. ....
Specialty ....
....